1. Introduction

A number of international trade models have now been developed that account for imperfect competition. Although some of these models provide insight into situations where trade protection may be welfare improving, most indicate that imperfect competition provides additional sources of gains from trade. Many of these gains result from the "pro-competitive" effect of trade: import competition increases the perceived elasticity of demand for domestic firms, leading them to reduce their markups of price over marginal cost.[1]

Applied general equilibrium models suggest that these effects may be important quantitatively. Harris (1984) and Cox and Harris (1985) perform a number of simulations of trade liberalization experiments calibrated for 1976 Canadian data. They find that the estimated welfare gains based on models incorporating imperfect competition are substantially greater than the estimated gains based on the corresponding perfectly competitive model. Similarly, in a study of the potential impact of the Canada-United States Free Trade Agreement, Brown and Stern's (1989) model suggests that the pro-competitive effects of Canadian tariff reductions may be quite strong in many Canadian industries.

Early econometric studies analyzing the impact of trade on market power employ the mark-up of price over average variable cost as a measure of non-competitive behavior. These studies generally find that import competition reduces average cost markups, particularly in domestically concentrated industries.[2] Economic theory, however, predicts

---

[1] See Markusen (1981).
[2] See, for example, Caves et al. (1980), Jacquemin et al. (1980), Pugel (1980), de Melo and Urata(1986), and Domowitz et al. (1986) and Katics and Petersen (1994).

that import competition reduces the mark-up of price over *marginal* cost, which is not directly observable. More recent studies draw on the work of Roberts (1984) and Hall (1988) to estimate price-marginal cost mark-ups from equations derived from profit maximizing conditions. Three studies apply this approach to plant-level data to analyze the impact of trade reform on competition in developing countries. Levinsohn (1993) finds that price-marginal cost mark-ups fell in Turkish industries where trade was liberalized, and increased in industries where trade protection was increased. Similarly, Harrison (1994) finds that mark-ups are negatively related to import competition in the Cote d'Ivoire, and Krishna and Mitra (1998) present evidence that mark-ups fell during the trade reform period in India.

This paper estimates price-marginal cost ratios using detailed establishment-level data for manufacturing industries in Canada during the 1970s. This period of study was chosen due to the considerable variation in trade and trade protection across industries as well as the increase in trade that took place between the early 1970s and the late 1970s. In 1970, average tariff rates for individual 2-digit industries ranged from 5.2% to 50.9%.[3] As a result of the Kennedy Round of trade negotiations, begun in 1966, the average tariff level for Canadian manufacturing fell from 10.7% in 1970 to 7.8% in 1978.[4] The share of domestic consumption of manufactures that was accounted for by imports rose from 26% in 1971 to 32.6% in 1979.[5] While this increase in import competition was not as substantial as that which occurred in the developing countries discussed above, it was

---

[3] Baldwin and Gorecki (1986: 7). Table 1 provides the average import intensity levels for the major industry groups.
[4] Baldwin and Gorecki (1986: 7).
[5] Baldwin and Gorecki (1986: 8). Imports in Canada increased even more dramatically during the 1990s, beginning in 1993. The data necessary to analyze this time period, however, were not available at the time the study was begun.

4

nonetheless significant and has been analyzed to evaluate the effect of international trade

on various aspects of the Canadian economy.[6]

The relationship between mark-ups and imports is estimated for two separate

cross-sections: the early 1970s and the late 1970s. In addition, the data for the two

periods are combined to analyze the impact of changes in import competition on mark-ups

over time. The primary conclusion that can be drawn from the analysis is that there is no

consistent evidence that import competition reduced the market power of firms operating

in the Canadian market during this period.

2. Empirical Framework

2.1 Estimating Price-Marginal Cost Ratios

Profit-maximization with respect to output yields the following relationship

between price and marginal cost:

$$\frac{P_{it}}{MC_{it}} = \left[1 + \frac{s_{it}\theta_{it}}{\eta_{it}}\right]^{-1} \equiv \beta_{it}, \tag{1}$$

where s_{it} is the market share of the firm, η_{it} is the market elasticity of demand in industry

i, and θ_{it} is the conjectural variations parameter $\left(= \partial Q_t / \partial q_{it}\right)$. As defined above, β_{it} is

the profit-maximizing ratio of price to marginal cost. The estimated value of this

parameter can be used to calculate the Lerner index, the mark-up of price over marginal

cost:

$$\frac{P - MC}{P} = 1 - \frac{1}{\beta}.$$

---

[6] See, for example, Baldwin and Gorecki (1986) and Caves (1990).

To estimate price-marginal cost ratios, I follow the approach employed by Levinsohn (1993). Consider the production function for a representative firm i:

$$q_{it} = \phi_{it} f(L_{it}) \qquad (2)$$

where L_{it} is a vector of j factors of production, f is a function common to all firms in the industry, and ϕ_{it} is a firm- and period-specific productivity shock that is assumed to follow a random walk:

$$\phi_{it} = \phi_{i,t-1} + \varepsilon_{it,,}$$

$$\varepsilon_{it} \approx N(0, \sigma^2).$$

Furthermore, it is assumed that ε_{it} is composed of a time-specific productivity shock that is common to all firms within a given industry and a productivity shock that is specific to the individual firm:

$$\varepsilon_{it} = \lambda_t + \mu_{it}.$$

To derive an estimating equation for β_{it}, totally differentiate (2),

$$dq_{it} = \phi_{it}\left[\sum_j \left(\partial f_{it} / \partial L_{jit}\right)dL_{jit}\right] + f_{it}(\lambda_t + \mu_{it}). \qquad (3)$$

Profit-maximization with respect to input markets implies that the firm employs each input until its marginal revenue product is equal to its price. Thus,

$$\phi_{it} P_{it} \frac{\partial f_{it}}{\partial L_{ijt}} \beta^{-1}{}_{it} = w_{ijt}, \qquad (4)$$

Solving (4) for $(\partial f_{it} / \partial L_{it})$ and substituting it into (3) yields:

$$dq_{it} = \beta_{it} \sum_j \frac{w_{ijt}}{P_t} dL_{ijt} + f_{it}(\lambda_t + \mu_{it}). \qquad (5)$$

Thus, β_{it} can be estimated by estimating the relationship between changes in output and factor price-weighted changes in inputs.

Price-marginal cost mark-ups are estimated for individual Canadian industries at the 3-digit Standard Industrial Classification (SIC) level for two years during the early 1970s and two years during the late 1970s. Following Levinsohn, three econometric issues are addressed. First, the term λ_t is modeled as a time-period fixed effect.[7] Second, the output price, p_t, is potentially endogenous since an individual firm (and shocks affecting that firm) may affect the industry price level. To address this concern, the wholesale price index is used as an instrument for the industry-level price index. The final concern is that the disturbance term of (5), $f_{it}(\lambda_t + \mu_{it})$, is heteroskedastic owing to the presence of the f_{it} term, which is a function of firm size. To address this issue, it is assumed in the estimation that the variance of the disturbance is proportional to the square of labor expenditures.

2.2 Estimating the Relationship between Price-Cost Ratios and Import Competition

In the second stage of the analysis, the impact of imports on price-marginal cost ratios is estimated. A negative relationship between trade and price-cost margins is indicated by a number of models, including Chamberlinian trade models (e.g., Krugman (1979)), Cournot models with free entry and exit (e.g., Dixit and Norman (1980)), and Cournot models with segmented markets (e.g., Brander (1981)). The relationship between price-cost ratios, imports and other explanatory variables can be expressed as:

---

[7] It is likely that λ_t is correlated with the changes in inputs. In this case, the fixed effects specification will lead to unbiased and consistent, but inefficient estimates. An alternative approach is to employ

$$\beta_h = \sum_k \gamma_k x_{hk} + v_h, \tag{6}$$

where β_h is the ratio of price to marginal cost for industry h, x is a vector of industry characteristics, including a measure of import competition, and v_h is the disturbance term, assumed to have a zero mean and constant variance of σ_v^2.

Studies specifically deriving the relationship between imports and price-cost margins have found that the appropriate empirical specification includes the interaction between imports and measures of the competitiveness of domestic suppliers.[8] This is because import competition can be expected to have the greatest impact on industries where domestic market conditions are such that competition would otherwise be weak. It is well known that it is difficult to capture differences in market structure by a single measure (or a manageable set of measures).[9] The four-firm concentration ratio is the most frequently employed indicator of domestic competition for studies of import competition and profitability and is therefore used here for comparability.[10]

In addition, owing to the high correlation between imports and exports (see below), it is important to control for the potential impact of exports so that the impact of imports can be isolated. Theoretical models lead to ambiguous predictions about the impact of exports on price-cost mark-ups. Suppose, for example, that export markets are

---

instrumental variables estimation although, as discussed by Levinsohn, appropriate instruments are not readily available.

[8] See the discussion in Caves (1985).

[9] See Bresnahan (1989) for a discussion of this issue.

[10] For previous versions of the paper, the model was also estimated using market share turnover between 1970 and 1980 as a measure of domestic competition. This variable is measured as the percentage shift of market share from declining establishments to growing establishments. The results were not substantially altered.

more competitive than domestic markets. In other words, domestic firms perceive higher elasticities of demand in export markets, resulting in lower mark-ups on exports than on domestic output. With segmented markets, it will be profitable for domestic firms to export as long as marginal revenue exceeds marginal cost. With constant marginal costs, the mark-up on domestic output is unchanged. With increasing marginal costs, however, the mark-up on domestic output actually increases. Since estimated mark-ups reflect a weighted average of the mark-ups on domestic output and exports, the net impact of exporting on mark-ups is ambiguous under this scenario.

The fact that price-marginal cost ratios are estimated (with error) rather than observed raises the issue of heteroskedasticity. Replacing β_h with $\hat{\beta}_h$, we have the following equation,

$$\hat{\beta}_h = \sum_k \gamma_k x_{hk} + \omega_h, \qquad (6\ ')$$

where $\omega_h = v_h + \xi_h$, and ξ_h is the estimation error of $\hat{\beta}_h$. The disturbance term is likely to be heteroskedastic owing to the fact that the variance of ξ_h is not constant across industries. Equation 6' is therefore estimated using feasible generalized least squares (GLS) following the procedure described in Appendix A.

3. Data

Price-marginal cost ratios are estimated for individual Canadian industries at the 3 digit Standard Industrial Classification (SIC) level over the periods 1971-2 and 1978-9 (based on changes from 1970-1 and 1971-2 for the first period and 1977-1978 and 1978-9 for the second period). Data for two years are combined for each estimate to reduce the sensitivity of the estimates to the particular year chosen as well as to increase the number of observations for each 3-digit industry.

To estimate equation (5), price and quantity data are required for output and factors of production. Five factors of production were initially considered: production workers, non-production workers, materials, fuel, and capital. Establishment-level data were obtained from the annual Census of Manufactures survey for: value of manufacturing production, hours worked by production workers, number of non-production workers, value of materials used in manufacturing production, and expenditures on fuel and energy. This survey covers every establishment assigned to the manufacturing sector. However, only establishments for which manufacturing activity accounts for at least 90% of total activity and for which there were no missing data for at least two consecutive years are included in the estimation. In addition, the analysis for each time period is based on the industries that had at least 20 observations. The final sample for which all data are available (including the international trade variables and other industry characteristics) consists of 97 industries for 1971-2 and 99 industries for 1978-9.

Data for capital investment were obtained from the Statistics Canada Capital Expenditures Survey. When the capital expenditures file was merged with the Census of Manufactures file, however, the sample size was significantly reduced. Preliminary analysis indicated that including capital as a factor of production did not significantly alter the estimates of the mark-ups for the sample of plants for which capital data were available.[11] Capital was therefore not included as a factor of production in the estimates below so that a larger sample could be used.

_____

[11] The correlations between the mark-ups estimated with and without capital were 97.8% and 98.8% for 1971 and 1979, respectively.

Quantities for production, materials, and fuel were computed by dividing the values of these variables by industry-level price indices. These indices were obtained from the KLEMS database, made available through the Input-Output division of Statistics Canada. Industry-level wages and salaries were calculated for each 3-digit SIC code by dividing total wages earned by production workers by the number of hoursworked and by dividing total salaries earned by nonproduction workers by the number of non-production workers.

Data on imports and exports at the 3-digit SIC level were obtained from the publication, Commodity Trade by Industrial Sector, Historical Summary, 1966-1983, published by the Department of Regional Industrial Expansion, Canada. Both the import and export data were corrected for re-exports. Import intensity is defined as the share of domestic consumption accounted for by imports, where domestic consumption is calculated as (domestic shipments- exports + imports). Export intensity is defined as the ratio of exports to shipments. The shipments data were obtained from the Statistics Canada publication Manufacturing Industries in Canada

Table 1 summarizes the trade data by major manufacturing groups for the 3-digit industries considered in this study.[12] Both import and export intensities increased in almost every major industry group.[13] As a result, the pattern of trade across industries is similar for both periods. This suggests, unfortunately, that it may be difficult to distinguish a differential impact of increased trade over the period on markups. The industries with the greatest import intensities in both the 1971-2 and the 1978-9 periods are leather, textiles, knitting mills, primary metals, machinery, transportation equipment, electrical

---

[12] The data in this table represent only the 3-digit industries used in this study and therefore do not correspond directly to trade data calculated at the 2-digit level.

equipment, and chemicals. Three of these industries, primary metals, machinery, and transportation equipment, are also among the industries with the largest export intensities. The correlations between import and export intensities are 0.55 and 0.50 for the 1971-2 and 1978-9 periods, respectively.

The data were provided by the Micro-Economic Analysis Division of Statistics Canada unless otherwise specified.

4. Results

4.1 Estimates of Price-Marginal Cost Ratios

Before discussing the results with respect to import competition, it is useful to summarize the estimates of the price-marginal cost ratios. The number of observations employed in the estimations ranged from 20 to 1370 for the individual 3-digit industries. Table 2 reports the summary statistics for both the 1971-2 and 1978-9 periods. The mean estimated price-marginal cost ratio for 1971-2 is 1.15 while the mean estimate for 1978-9 is 1.09, indicating a fall in the average mark-up from 12.7% to 8.6%. This is within the range of estimates reported by other studies based on plant-level data. Harrison (1994), for example, reports an average mark-up across sectors of 8%.

Owing to the significant increase in trade during the 1970s, the general reduction in estimated price-marginal cost ratios during this period is consistent with the hypothesis that trade increases competition. In addition, the proportion of ratios that is statistically significantly greater than one fell from 70% to 44%. The increase in competition is not

---

[13] The exceptions are petroleum and coal, where import intensity fell and knitting mills where export intensities fell.

uniform, however. Panel C of Table 2 provides summary statistics for the change in price-marginal cost ratios. Although 29% of the industries experienced a statistically significant decline in their mark-ups, 15% actually experienced a statistically significant increase.[14]

Table 3 summarizes the 3-digit mark-ups according to 2-digit industry groups. Six industries had average ratios above the median for both the early 1970s and the late 1970s: tobacco products, electrical products, non-metal mineral products, petroleum and coal, rubber and plastic, and miscellaneous; while six industries had average ratios below the median for both periods: paper and related products, wood products, clothing, printing and publishing, knitting mills, and food and beverages.

4.2 Cross-sectional Analysis: Benchmark Model

Table 4 presents the cross-sectional GLS results of equation (6') estimated separately for 1971-2 and 1978-9. The question here is whether domestically concentrated industries with high levels of import competition have lower price-marginal cost margins than domestically concentrated industries with low import competition. The coefficient on the interaction between imports and concentration is negative as predicted for both time periods, although not statistically significant. As will be discussed more fully below, this relatively weak relationship between mark-ups and import competition may reflect, in part, the simultaneity problem that high mark-ups attract imports.

The relationship between mark-ups and export intensity is negative for all of the equations in Table 4, although it is not statistically significant. With respect to domestic concentration, the results indicate that concentration did not have a significant impact on price-marginal cost ratios for the 1971-2 period. It did, however, have a significant

---

[14] To estimate the correct standard errors, the data were combined for the two periods and a dummy

positive impact for the 1978-9 period. It is interesting that the estimated effect is stronger for the 1978-9 period. Due to the increase in international trade during the 1970s, one could predict that the level of domestic concentration would have been less important in the late 1970s than in the early 1970s. This result may reflect the weakness of using a single measure to capture the complex variations in market structure.

For purposes of comparison, Domowitz et al. (1988) find that concentration has a small, but significant, positive impact on estimated price-marginal cost mark-ups for U.S. manufacturing industries. When the analysis is performed for different types of industries, however, they find that the relationship between concentration and mark-ups is strong for consumer goods and durable goods industries, but insignificant for producer goods and non-durable goods industries. In addition, they find that the relationship varies over the business cycle.

4.3 Instrumental Variables Estimates

As mentioned above, there is a potential simultaneity between price-cost ratios and imports. If imports are determined endogenously, then the GLS estimates will be biased. Instrumental variables estimates are reported in columns (3) and (4) in Table 4. Appropriate instruments are correlated with imports, but uncorrelated with the error term of equation (6'). The set of instruments consists of the nominal tariff rate and dummy variables for natural resource and labor-intensive industries.[15] Interactions between these

---

variable was employed to capture the change in mark-ups with the corresponding standard error.
[15] The tariff data were generously provided by Larry Schembri. These data were defined according to the input-output "PL" level classification and concorded to SIC codes. The labor and natural resource dummy variables are based on the OECD (1987) taxonomy adapted for the Canadian economy by Baldwin and Raffiquzzaman (1994).

instruments and concentration are also included as instruments for the estimation equations that include the interaction between concentration and imports. An alternative set of regressions was estimated using the effective rate of protection as an instrument in place of the nominal tariff rate. The results were very similar to those discussed below.[16]

As discussed by Bound, Jaeger and Baker (1995), the finite sample bias of IV estimates may be quantitatively important when the correlation between the endogenous variables and the instruments is weak. In particular, a good approximation of the bias of IV estimates relative to OLS estimates is provided by $(1/F)$, where F is the F statistic for the instruments in the first stage regression. The F-statistics for the instruments employed here range from to 2.1 to 4.4, indicating that the potential bias of the IV estimates is small relative to the OLS estimates.

The IV results are reported in columns (3) and (4).[17] The IV estimates differ in magnitude from the OLS estimates and are estimated with larger standard errors. The implications of the results, however, are similar. Based on the Hausman test, the hypothesis that the two sets of estimates are the same cannot be rejected at the 5% level of significance for any of the estimating equations. Therefore, the hypothesis that imports are exogenous cannot be rejected.

4.4 The Impact of Multinational Corporations

In this section, the role of multinational corporations in determining the relationship between import competition and mark-ups is examined. This is motivated by theoretical and applied general equilibrium work by Markusen et al. (1995) that suggests

---

[16] Effective rates of protection measures were generously provided by John Baldwin for 1970 and 1978.

that the pro-competitive effect of trade may be dampened by the presence of multinational corporations. This is because an increase in imports may actually increase the market share and mark-up of foreign-owned firms operating in the domestic market if imports originate from the parent company. In this case, trade liberalization will not necessarily have the *overall* pro-competitive effect that has been emphasized in much of the trade policy literature.

A related issue is intra-firm trade. Increases in imports may be due, in part, to increases in intermediate goods imports within the same firm. In this case, an observed increase in imports will not necessarily represent an increase in competition. These are potentially important issues in Canada. It has been estimated that foreign-controlled importers accounted for approximately 70% of Canadian imports in 1978.[18] Furthermore, approximately two-thirds of the total imports by foreign-controlled firms were intra-affiliate imports in 1986, the first year for which this type of information is available.[19]

To investigate the impact of multinational corporations on the potential pro-competitive effects of trade, the estimation equation is augmented to include an interaction term between imports, domestic concentration, and a measure of foreign ownership. The prediction is that the coefficient on this variable will be positive, indicating that foreign ownership weakens the potential for imports to increase competition in domestically concentrated industries. The percentage of industry imports that were imported by foreign controlled firms (FIMP) is used as the measure of the importance of foreign ownership. This variable is only available for 1978.[20] The 1978 value is used for both time periods

---

[17] The IV estimates are also based on GLS estimation to account for the fact that the mark-ups are estimated with error.
[18] Statistics Canada (1978).
[19] Mersereau (1990: 403).
[20] Statistics Canada (1978).

based on the assumption that it was relatively stable over time.[21] Unfortunately, detailed

data on intra-affiliate imports are not available. They are likely, however, to be correlated

with FIMP.

The results of the augmented regression are reported in columns (2) and (6) in

Table 5. The coefficient on the interaction between imports, concentration, and foreign

ownership is positive as predicted, although not statistically significant. Comparing these

results to the benchmark model (repeated in columns (1) and (5)), the coefficient on the

interaction between imports and concentration becomes larger in absolute value and is

marginally significant at the 10% level for the 1971-2 period.   These results provide

some, albeit weak, evidence that the potential disciplining effect of imports is diminished in

industries with a relatively high degree of foreign ownership. This is consistent with the

prediction of Markusen et al. (1995), and has not previously been tested.

4.5 Additional Control Variables

In this section, the estimation equation is augmented further to include additional

control variables. The first is demand growth, which is defined to be the industry-level

percentage change in demand during the relevant periods. For the 1971-2 period, for

example, it is the percentage change between 1972 and 1970.[22]

The other additional control variable is a measure of entry into the industry. It is

defined as the mean over the period 1970 to 1982 of the proportion of new entrants in a

---

[21] Alternatively, the equations were estimated using a dummy variable indicating whether the value of this variable was greater than the mean. The results were not significantly affected.

[22] Domestic demand is defined as (domestic shipments-exports+imports) and is calculated at the 2-digit level to minimize potential endogeneity problems.   The data were taken from the Statistics Canada publication, Manufacturing Trade and Measures, 1966-1984. Quantities were deflated by industry-level price indices calculated from the KLEMS database.

year.[23] [24] It is hypothesized that mark-ups will be lower when new entry is relatively easy. The entry variable is also interacted with concentration and the interaction between imports and concentration since the effect of concentration on mark-ups should be reduced when there is potential entry in the industry.

The results are presented in columns (3), (4), (7), and (8) in Table 5. The coefficients for the growth variables are not statistically significant. Nor are the entry variables for the 1971-2 period. For the 1978-9 period, the interaction between entry and concentration is negative and significant, suggesting that entry reduces mark-ups in concentrated industries. The coefficient on entry alone is positive and significant. The overall impact of entry on mark-ups, however, is insignificant.[25] The important point to note from these results is that the conclusions with respect to the international trade variables are not affected by the addition of these variables.

4.6 Analysis Based on Changes Between 1971-2 and 1978-9

A well-known problem with cross-sectional analysis of industry performance is that there are likely to be important industry characteristics that are either unobservable or difficult to measure.[26] If unobserved characteristics are correlated with the explanatory variables, then the cross-sectional estimates will be biased. If unobserved industry effects are relatively time invariant, estimation based on changes over time can control for these fixed effects.

---

[23] These data were generously provided by John Baldwin.
[24] Alternative specifications were estimated using the capital/revenue ratio and a product differentiation dummy variable as measures of barriers to entry. The results with respect to the international trade variables were not affected.
[25] The coefficients on entry are small and insignificant when the interaction terms are not entered into the regressions.
[26] See Bresnahan (1989) and Schmalensee (1989) for discussions.

Table 6 presents the results based on changes between the 1978-9 and the 1971-2 periods. Unless otherwise specified, all variables are expressed in terms of differences between these two periods. Following Katics and Petersen (1994), it is assumed that all industry characteristics other than the international trade variables are constant over time. This includes the domestic concentration ratio.[27]

The interaction between the concentration ratio and changes in imports is included to determine whether import competition had a differential impact between concentrated and unconcentrated industries.[28] The coefficient on this interaction term is positive and marginally significant at the 10% level. Therefore, in contrast to the cross-sectional results, the results here indicate that imports may have actually increased mark-ups in domestically concentrated industries. The implications of these results are not changed when the estimation controls for the impact of multinational imports (column (2)) or differences in growth rates between the two periods (column (3)).

To pursue these results further, the equations were estimated for the subsample of industries for which the 1971-2 price-marginal cost ratio was statistically significantly greater than one. These are the industries where one would expect increased import competition to have the greatest effect. The results were generally the same as those reported in Table 6: there is no evidence that increased imports led to a reduction in mark-ups.

These findings are inconsistent with the hypothesis that imports increase competition in the domestic market and are in contrast to the results of similar studies that are based on developing countries (e.g., Levinsohn (1993) and Harrison (1994)). One

---

[27] The domestic concentration ratio is relatively constant. The sample mean of this variable falls from 43.7 to 43.2 between 1970 and 1980, and the correlation between the two periods is 0.94.
[28] The average of the 1970 and 1980 concentration ratios is employed to calculate this variable.

potential reason for the differences in these results is that the trade liberalizations in Turkey and the Cote d'Ivoire were much more dramatic than the Canadian experience of the 1970s. The weighted average tariff for the sectors included in Harrison's study of the Cote d'Ivoire, for example, fell from 102% to 72% during the sample period. In contrast, the average tariff level for Canadian manufacturing fell from 10.7 in 1970 to 7.8 in 1978.[29]

Although small relative to trade liberalizations in developing countries, the increase in import competition in Canada during the 1970s was nonetheless significant. Thus, one would expect that changes in imports would have had an impact on price-cost margins. As discussed above, however, trade increased in almost all industries. Therefore, the results may reflect a difficulty in distinguishing a differential impact across industries of increased trade over the period.

Another possible explanation is that the level of aggregation is too broad to capture the impact of import competition. Products within 3-digit industries may face different levels of protection. In addition, even within more narrowly defined industries, individual firms may respond differently to trade. Thus, detailed firm-level analysis may provide a more complete understanding of the potential pro-competitive effects of imports.

An interesting result from Table 6 is that the coefficient for changes in exports is negative and statistically significant at the 5% level for all four estimations. The negative relationship between mark-ups and export orientation reinforces the cross-sectional analysis and suggests that participation in export markets places competitive pressure on domestic exporting firms. As discussed above (section 2.2), however, this does not

---

[29] Baldwin and Gorecki (1986: 7).

necessarily imply that mark-ups on domestic output fall since the mark-ups reflect a weighted average of the mark-ups on domestic output and exports.

5. Conclusion

This paper estimates price-*marginal* cost mark-ups for Canadian manufacturing industries in order to assess the impact of import competition on domestic market power. The results are mixed. There is some weak cross-sectional evidence to suggest that imports reduced market power in domestically concentrated industries. *Changes* in imports between the two periods, however, had a (weak) positive impact on mark-ups in concentrated industries. One possible explanation for this finding is that trade may have differential impacts among firms within industries. Detailed firm-level analysis may therefore provide a more complete understanding of the impact of imports on competition.

6. Appendix A

The disturbance term of equation 6' is $\omega_h = v_h + \xi_{h,}$. It is assumed that

$E(v_h, \xi_h) = 0$. The variance of $\omega_h, \sigma_\omega^2$, is therefore equal to $\sigma_v^2 + \sigma_{\xi h}^2$. Let w_h

represent the residuals from an OLS regression of equation 6'. The variance of ω_h can be

estimated as follows.

$$p\lim\left(\frac{\sum w_h^2}{n-k}\right) = \sigma_v^2 + \frac{\sum \text{var}\left(\Delta\hat{\beta}_h\right)}{n-k} \tag{A1}$$

Thus,

$$\hat{\sigma}_v = \left(\frac{\sum w_h^2}{n-k}\right) - \frac{\sum \hat{\text{var}}\left(\Delta\hat{\beta}_h\right)}{n-k} \tag{A2}$$

The first term on the right hand side of equation (A2) can be calculated from the residuals

of equation 6' and the second term can be derived from the variance estimates of equation

(5) for the individual industries. Equation 6' is then estimated using feasible generalized

least squares where the observations are divided by $\sqrt{\hat{\sigma}_v + \hat{\text{var}}\left(\Delta\hat{\beta}_h\right)}$.

Table 1: Mean Import and Export Intensities by Major Industry Group

Industry	Import intensity		Export intensity	
	1971-2	1978-9	1971-2	1978-9
Food and beverage industries	0.090	0.130	0.142	0.172
Tobacco products industries	0.016	0.022	0.008	0.008
Rubber and plastic products	0.179	0.227	0.048	0.106
Leather industries	0.264	0.351	0.076	0.095
Textile industries	0.232	0.280	0.041	0.059
Knitting mills	0.184	0.235	0.018	0.014
Clothing industries	0.090	0.130	0.098	0.099
Wood industries	0.082	0.127	0.184	0.245
Furniture and fixture industries	0.060	0.101	0.045	0.094
Paper and allied industries	0.072	0.087	0.259	0.266
Printing and publishing	0.145	0.162	0.022	0.034
Primary metal industries	0.233	0.301	0.440	0.458
Metal fabricating industries	0.135	0.150	0.054	0.083
Machinery industries	0.630	0.668	0.344	0.383
Transportation equipment	0.359	0.362	0.372	0.385
Electrical product industries	0.256	0.348	0.111	0.155
Non-Metallic mineral products	0.182	0.193	0.133	0.163
Petroleum and coal products	0.079	0.033	0.043	0.085
Chemical products	0.214	0.251	0.086	0.127
Miscellaneous manufacturing	0.370	0.408	0.155	0.165

Note: These data summarize the import and export intensities of the 3-digit industries included in this study and therefore do not correspond directly to trade data calculated at the 2-digit level.

Table 2: Summary Statistics
Price-Marginal Cost Ratios

	# Obs	Mean	Standard Deviation	Implied Mark-up
Panel A: 1971-2 Period				
Full Sample	97	1.146	0.182	0.127
Significantly greater than one	68	1.225	0.134	0.184
Not significantly different from one	24	1.012	0.072	0.012
Significantly less than one	5	0.724	0.174	-0.381
Panel B: 1978-9 Period				
Full Sample	99	1.094	0.219	0.086
Significantly greater than one	44	1.262	0.149	0.208
Not significantly different from one	42	1.023	0.129	0.022
Significantly less than one	13	0.756	0.103	-0.323
Panel C: **Change between two periods**				
Full Sample	97	-0.057	0.279	-
Significant increases	15	0.329	0.196	-
No significant change	54	-0.020	0.178	-
Significant decrease	28	-0.335	0.171	-

Note: Significance refers to statistical significance at the 5% level.

Table 3: Mean Mark-ups for Major Industry Groups

	#Obs. (a)	1971-2		1978-9	
		Price/cost ratio	Implied mark-up	Price/cost ratio	Implied mark-up
Food and beverage industries	9	1.063	0.059	1.074	0.069
Tobacco products industries	1	1.374	0.272	1.641	0.391
Rubber and plastic products	2	1.130	0.115	1.272	0.214
Leather industries	3	1.099	0.090	1.215	0.177
Textile industries	7	1.113	0.101	1.076	0.070
Knitting mills	2	1.108	0.098	0.999	-0.001
Clothing industries	6	1.089	0.082	0.959	-0.043
Wood industries	6	1.091	0.083	1.100	0.091
Furniture and fixture industries	4	1.067	0.063	1.193	0.162
Paper and allied industries	3 (4)	1.092	0.084	0.851	-0.175
Printing and publishing	3	1.027	0.027	1.012	0.012
Primary metal industries	7	1.065	0.061	1.127	0.113
Metal fabricating industries	8	1.179	0.152	1.032	0.031
Machinery industries	3	1.285	0.222	1.098	0.089
Transportation equipment	5	1.112	0.101	1.137	0.121
Electrical product industries	6	1.247	0.198	1.185	0.156
Non-metallic mineral products	8 (9)	1.250	0.200	1.105	0.095
Petroleum and coal products	2	1.158	0.136	1.238	0.192
Chemical products	7	1.282	0.220	1.028	0.027
Miscellaneous manufacturing	5	1.183	0.155	1.172	0.146

(a) The number of 3-digit industries included in each major industry group. The numbers in parentheses indicate the number of industries for 1978-9 when different from the 1971-2 period.

Table 4: Results

| | GLS Estimates | | IV Estimates | |
	1971-2	1978-9	1971-2	1978-9
Imports	0.444 (0.228)	0.423 (0.252)	1.045 (0.710)	-0.076 (0.770)
Imports*C4	-0.436 (0.432)	-0.687 (0.494)	-1.255 (0.993)	-0.468 (1.107)
C4	0.129 (0.117)	0.453* (0.157)	0.292 (0.211)	0.410 (0.285)
Exports	-0.084 (0.111)	-0.182 (0.128)	-0.134 (0.195)	-0.009 (0.219)
Constant	1.060* (0.055)	0.905* (0.073)	0.955* (0.124)	0.985* (0.163)
# Observations	97	99	97	99
Hausman Statistic	-	-	0.870	1.017

Results are based on feasible generalized least squares estimation following the procedure described in Appendix A.

Standard errors are in parentheses.
* Statistically significant at the 5% level.

Table 5: Extended Analysis

| | 1971-2 | | | | 1978-9 | | | |
	(1)	(2)	(3)	(4)	(5)	(6)	(7)	(8)
Imports	0.444 (0.228)	0.525* (0.230)	0.523* (0.230)	0.497* (0.248)	0.423* (0.252)	0.434* (0.255)	0.440* (0.257)	0.278 (0.271)
Imports*C4	-0.436 (0.432)	-1.064 (0.573)	-0.985 (0.575)	-0.435 (0.471)	-0.687 (0.494)	-0.815 (0.653)	-0.816 (0.656)	-0.680 (0.509)
Imports*C4* FIMP	-	0.718 (0.481)	0.676 (0.480)	-	-	0.248 (0.543)	0.242 (0.546)	-
Imports*C4* entry	-	-	-	-1.693 (6.173)	-	-	-	8.163 (7.446)
C4	0.129 (0.117)	0.174 (0.119)	0.179 (0.119)	0.073 (0.189)	0.453* (0.157)	0.424* (0.159)	0.429* (0.162)	0.806* (0.223)
C4*entry	-	-	-	1.419 (3.785)	-	-	-	-9.894* (4.591)
Entry	-	-	-	-0.841 (1.360)	-	-	-	3.769* (1.604)
Exports	-0.084 (0.111)	-0.092 (0.110)	-0.083 (0.110)	-0.089 (0.115)	-0.182 (0.128)	-0.177 (0.128)	-0.171 (0.131)	-0.192 (0.127)
Growth	-	-	-0.347 (0.270)	-	-	-	-0.043 (0.191)	-
Constant	1.060* (0.055)	1.046* (0.055)	1.089* (0.065)		0.905* (0.073)	0.915* (0.074)	0.909* (0.074)	0.734* (0.123)
# Observations	97	95	95	95	99	97	97	97

Note: Results are based on feasible generalized least squares estimation following the procedure described in Appendix A.

Standard errors are in parentheses.
* Statistically significant at the 5% level.

Table 6: Results based on Changes between 1971-2 and 1978-9

	(1)	(2)	(3)
Import intensity	-1.159 (1.107)	-1.023 (1.112)	-1.166 (1.134)
Imports*C4	3.730 (2.151)	3.281 (3.599)	3.888 (3.712)
Imports*C4*FIMP	-	0.499 (4.218)	0.262 (4.244)
Export intensity	-1.111* (0.486)	-1.093* (0.484)	-1.128* (0.488)
Demand growth	-	-	-0.166 (0.239)
Constant	-0.046 (0.034)	-0.054 (0.034)	-0.055 (0.034)
# Observations	97	95	95

Note: Results are based on feasible generalized least squares estimation following the procedure described in Appendix A.

Standard errors are in parentheses.

* Statistically significant at the 5% level.

References

Baldwin, John and Paul Gorecki. (1986). *The Role of Scale in Canada-U.S. Productivity Differences in the Manufacturing Sector 1970-1979*. Toronto: University of Toronto Press.

Baldwin, John and M. Rafiquzzaman. (1994). Structural Change in the Canadian Manufacturing Sector: 1970-1990. Research Paper Series #61, Analytical Studies Branch, Statistics Canada, Ottawa, Canada.

Bound, John, David A. Jaeger and Regina M. Baker. (1995). Problems with Instrumental Variables Estimation when the Correlation Between the Instruments and the Endogenous Explanatory Variable is Weak. *Journal of the American Statistical Association* 90(430): 443-50.

Brander, James. (1981). Intra-Industry Trade in Identical Commodities. *Journal of International Economics*, 11(1): 1-14.

Bresnahan, Timothy. (1989). Empirical Studies of Industries with Market Power. In Schmalensee and Willig (eds.), *Handbook of Industrial Organization*. The Netherlands: Elsevier Science Publishers.

Brown, Drusilla and Robert M. Stern. (1989). Computable General Equilibrium Estimates of the Gains from US-Canadian Trade Liberalization. In Greenaway et al. (eds.), *Economic Aspects of Regional Trading Arrangements*. New York: New York University Press.

Caves, Richard. (1985). International trade and industrial organization: problems solved and unsolved. *European Economic Review*. 28(3): 377-395.

Caves, Richard. (1990). *Adjustment to International Competition: Short-Run Relations of Prices, Trade Flows, and Inputs in Canadian Manufacturing Industries*. Ottawa: Economic Council of Canada, distributed by Minister of Supply and Services, Canada.

Caves, Richard, M.E. Porter and A.M. Spence. (1980). *Competition in the Open Economy: A Model Applied to Canada.* Cambridge MA: Harvard University Press.

Cox, David and Richard G. Harris. (1985). Trade Liberalization and Industrial Competitiveness: Some Estimates for Canada. *Journal of Political Economy* 93(1): 115-145.

Dixit, A. and V. Norman. (1980). *Theory of International Trade.* Cambridge: Cambridge University Press.

Domowitz, Ian, R. Glenn Hubbard, and Bruce C. Petersen. (1986) Business cycles and the relationship between concentration and price-cost margins. *Rand Journal of Economics* 17(1): 1-17.

Domowitz, Ian, R. Glenn Hubbard, and Bruce C. Petersen. (1988). Market Structure and Cyclical Fluctuations in U.S. Manufacturing. *Review of Economics and Statistics* 70(1): 55-66.

Geroski, P.A. and Jacquemin, A. (1981) Imports as Competitive Discipline. *Recherches Economique de Louvan* 47: 197-208.

Hall, Robert. (1988). The Relation between Price and Marginal Cost in U.S. Industry. *Journal of Political Economy* 96(5): 921-947.

Harris, Richard G. (1984). Applied General Equilibrium Analysis of Small Open Economies with Scale Economies and Imperfect Competition. *American Economic Review* 74(5): 1016-1032.

Harrison, Ann. (1994). Productivity, Imperfect Competition and Trade Reform: Theory and Evidence. *Journal of International Economics* 36(1-2): 53-73.

Jacquemin, A., E. de Ghellinck and C. Huveneers. (1980). Concentration and profitability in a small open economy. *Journal of Industrial Economics* 29(2): 131-144.

Katics, Michelle and Bruce Petersen. (1994). The Effect of Rising Import Penetration on Market Power: A Panel Data Study of US Manufacturing. *The Journal of Industrial Economics* 43(2): 277-286.

Krishna, Pravin and Devashish Mitra. (1998). Trade Liberalization, Market Discipline and Productivity Growth: New Evidence from India. *Journal of Development Economics* 56(2): 447-462.

Krugman, Paul. (1979). Increasing Returns, Monopolistic Competition, and Trade. *Journal of International Economics* 9(4): 469-479.

Levinsohn, James. (1993). Testing the imports-as-market-discipline hypothesis. *Journal of International Economics* 35(1-2): 1-22.

Markusen, James. (1981). Trade and the gains from trade with imperfect competition. *Journal of International Economics* 11(4): 531-551.

Markusen, James, Thomas Rutherford, and Linda Hunter. (1995). Trade Liberalization in a Multinational-dominated Industry. *Journal of International Economics* 38(1-2): 95-117.

Martins, Joaquim Oliveira, Stefano Scarpetta and Dirk Pilat. (1996). Mark-Up Ratios in Manufacturing Industries: Estimates for 14 OECD Countries. OECD Economics Department Working Papers, No. 162, Paris: OECD.

Melo, J. de and S. Urata. (1986). The influence of increased foreign competition on industrial concentration and profitability. *International Journal of Industrial Organization* 4(3): 287-304.

Mersereau, Barry. (1992). Characteristics of Canadian Importing Firms, 1978-1986. *Canadian Economic Observer* August.

OECD. (1987). *Structural Adjustment and Economic Performance*. Paris OECD.

Pugel, T.A. (1980). Foreign Trade and U.S. Market Performance. *Journal of Industrial Economics* 29(2): 119-130.

Roberts, Mark. (1984). Testing Oligopolistic Behavior. *International Journal of Industrial Organization* 2(4): 367-383.

Schmalensee, Richard. (1989). Inter-Industry Studies of Structure and Performance. In Schmalensee and Willig (eds), *Handbook of Industrial Organization*. The Netherlands: Elsevier Science Publishers.

Statistics Canada. (1978). *Canadian imports by domestic and foreign controlled enterprises, Catalogue 67-509, Occasional*. Ottawa: Minister of Supply and Services, Canada.